Slawston Rectory

Chapter One. The Rectory

I would like to tell you what an old English Rectory was like in the 1930's, as I experienced it. The house was built in 1859 and still stands today. Although it's no longer used as a rectory. I wish with all my heart that I could see it as it is today. I'm sure it has been brought up to date, but at the same time I hope some of its original beauty remains.

The church was called All Saints and it is still located in the village of Slawston, in Leicestershire. It dates back to the late 13th century, a time when the Church of England split from the Roman Catholic Church. So, it is very old. I remember that on each side of the church entrance door there were two stone faces, I think they were saints. With age those Saint's noses had worn off. I remember my nanny used to place her cigarette in the Saint's lips before we'd go inside the church. Sometimes my grandfather, the Reverend Charles Hanmer-Strudwick would catch nanny doing that and he would have a word with her. Nanny kept on doing it anyway.

The rectory was built on a large lot of land. It included a front garden, a kitchen garden, a large driveway with a spinney (now known as a wooded area), and had a large white gate facing the road with "Rectory" written on it. It had a large back yard with all sorts of brick rooms (wash house, pig sty, two were empty).

Outside the back door was a small room with one window which was never used in my time. Next to it was the wash house with a great big copper boiler built in the corner and a wooden table and a large mangel with two large wooden rollers which was turned by a handle to wring the water from the clothes. We had a grey cat that somehow got his tale caught in the rollers, and when the rollers were released his tail curled up in a ringlet. It stayed that way, poor thing. I guess Nanny gave it "Bob Martin's Powder". All of the animals were given that no matter what was wrong with them. That grey cat lived to be very old.

Once a week, Nanny would go outside, no matter the time of the year or the weather, and she would light the boiler with wood and coal and bring the water to a boil. She put a small blue bag in the boiler water which contained a blue powder. It was a way to keep the white clothes white when they were boiled. With a wooden pole, she would lift the boiled clothes out of the boiler and put them into a square tub to rinse them with cold water. I helped to put them through the wringer. She would then put the coloured clothes in the boiler water. Everything was hung up with pegs on ropes strung across the yard. This was done once a week. When she was done, Nanny had to ladle all the dirty water out of the boiler and put it down the drain hole in the floor. The floor sloped to the middle where the drain was. She worked very hard in her younger years when she was the maid for the family as well as having to look after me and my visiting cousins. Her name was Nora French and she lived to be 96 years old, such a wonderful lady.

At the bottom of the yard was a large building which housed two cars. My mom's Austin, which she called her, "Titch" and my grandparents' car which was a bigger Austin sedan. When my mother's car wouldn't start on damp cold days, she would take the spark plugs out and put them in the oven in the kitchen, and then it would start for her.

Next to that was a stable. A pig called Horris was kept in it. He grew to be a large, fat pig. But, because of Horris, during the war years, we lost all of our bacon food stamps. Nanny used to get Horris to lay on his back and she rubbed his tummy with straw. I got quite fond of Horris and I would sit on the straw and talk to him. I remember one incident when I was on leave from the Navy. I was in uniform, ready to go back to camp, and the pig came up to nuzzle against my leg. I didn't want slop on my black stockings, so I ran and Horris ran after me, down the driveway, into the street. A farm boy stood laughing at me. After I yelled at the farm boy, he chased Horris up the driveway to the pig sty. I never did live that one down.

The yard was entirely paved with bricks which sloped to the middle with drains.
On the side of the yard was a half wall, behind which the garbage was put and burned. There was no garbage pickup in those days. All food products were thrown right on the back garden for compost.

Also in this large yard was a coal house for the many fireplaces in the house. Next door to that was an outhouse. Lyme was put into the outhouse through the seat hole. It was never emptied because the lyme took care of all the waste.

Beside the outhouse was a huge wooden door in a brick wall (which had forged wrought iron hinges and an iron bar and slot to keep it closed). This led to the kitchen garden. My mum had a greenhouse and loved to grow rare plants. She tried to grow corn on the cob, which was not possible in England because of the damp weather. It got earwigs in it and it had to be burned. The kitchen garden was very large and my grandmother grew everything in it. She had a gardener, Harry Freston, who lived in the village. He was a dedicated worker. He would go out in the snow to pick brussel sprouts in the winter. We only had brussel sprouts in the wintertime.

Behind the kitchen garden, my grandmother had a large herbaceous garden which consisted of all perennials across the back, along the farmer's fence. I used to spend hours laying on a blanket looking in the garden for elves and fairies. When I was small I had read Hans Christian Anderson and Grimm's Fairy Tales. Being a child, I swore that I saw fairies. The old gardener

would shake his head but he never let me know that he doubted me. He was a real sweetheart. He was the only one who paid any attention to me. He had a crush on Nanny. As a child I had no one to play with, unless my cousins were visiting, or if my one friend Betty Cook was allowed out to play. I made up a game called Chemist shop (nowadays called a drug store). I took any clear glass bottles out of the garbage and filled them with the dirty wash water. I then coloured the water using crepe paper and I pretended I was a chemist. I spent hours outside sitting on a wooden box with another box propped up in front of me. The crepe paper made the water turn such pretty colours. I'd hold the clear glass bottles up towards the sky and watch as the pretty colours bled into the water.

Once I had an abscess in the front of my mouth, and my upper lip was swollen, it was very painful. For some reason Nanny used to tell me that because I was Canadian I was tough and so I was not allowed to cry. I was born in Canada, but when mummy returned to England with me, I was just three years old. At that time I was 12 years old. The abscess was so painful that I would go out into the garden to cry in secret. Harry always had a kind word for me. I was sent to the dentist in Market Harborough where my front teeth were drilled. And there was no freezing in those days. To this day I will never go to the dentist.

The entrance to the front of the house had steps, and a large door which led into a small brick porch with an arched ceiling and another front door. This door opened into a large hall with a circular staircase going up the left wall. At the top there was a landing that went all across the back of the house. The railing continued up along the back wall with wrought iron spindles which held up the heavy railing. The bedrooms and dressing rooms were all off of this landing.

At the end of the landing was my mother's room. It was a dressing room which had been made into a bedroom. Mum had a small bed, a wardrobe, and a dressing table with drawers. It had a window and a door that led into my grandparents 'bedroom. This was a large bedroom which had a fireplace. In there were two beds, a dressing table, and a large wardrobe. Nanny used to light the fire every morning before my grandparents got up, to warm the room. No central heating back then. It was from this room that one night Nanny came running down the stairs, shaking. She told us that she was in the bedroom lighting the fire and she felt someone behind her. She thought it was my Uncle Ben who was staying at the house at that time. She said, "Okay, Ben, I know you are there." But, when she turned around, she saw another uncle standing there in an RAF uniform, my Uncle Jack Strudwick. At that time, Uncle Jack was overseas. As it happened, a few days later, my grandmother got a telegram that he had been killed. He died the same day that Nanny saw him just for a moment. I will never forget Nanny's face. I was in the kitchen with my mother. Nanny was in quite a state so we didn't doubt her.

At the other end of the landing there was another bedroom where my Uncle Ben's wife, my auntie was dying of breast cancer at the young age of 33. She left behind two very young children, my cousins, Benito and her younger brother, David. At the very end of the landing was a small room where all of the Christmas decorations were kept. The bannisters were great for us kids to slide down. This was forbidden but, as kids, we did it anyway. At the bottom of the stairs was a large open hall. The dining room was off of it.

The dining room had beige walls and red curtains and a large dining table which could seat up to twenty people with the leaves in it. It didn't have table legs, just a huge strong mahogany pedestal beneath it. There was a sideboard, an upright piano, and a buffet table with drawers. Also in that room my grandmother had a writing desk. The room had French doors which opened out onto the front garden. The doors had a bay window either side. They had shutters made of wood with wrought iron bars that went across them to keep them closed. Hanging either side of the bay windows were heavy red velvet curtains. In the winter they were pulled across because of the cold air that otherwise came in. This room also had a fireplace for which Nanny had to haul coal in from outside and light every evening in the winter.

Next door to the dining room was the drawing room. It was the same size as the dining room and also had a fireplace, French doors which opened to the outside, and a large bay window with the same shutters down each side. In this room there were white walls and light blue velvet curtains. It also had two feather-filled couches and a white and blue patterned carpet. This room was not used very often. It had a grand piano which my mother loved to play.

A third room off of the hall, was my grandfather's study. It contained a desk, fireplace, and built-in bookcases on each side of the window, which looked out onto the kitchen garden. There were two leather wingback chairs by the fireplace.

To leave the front hall, you went through a blazer door. That is a single door that swings both ways. It was covered with thick green felt with rows of brass studs. This door led to four steps made of stone which Nanny used to sharpen the kitchen knives. The steps were worn in the middle but the knives were always sharp.

Nanny

At the bottom of the steps, to the right, was the kitchen. It had a brick coloured flagstone floor which Nanny always seemed to be on her knees scrubbing. There was a large table in the middle of the room covered with oilcloth. As kids, we used to eat most of our meals here with Nanny.

We were not allowed to eat in the dining room because we giggled. Remember, at this time, little children were to be seen and not heard.

Under the kitchen window was another table where the grandchildren were allowed to play board games. Nanny also had an old armchair to relax in whenever she could. On one wall was the fireplace with a wrought iron hook hanging from it to put a kettle or a pot on. The kettle was made of copper. My daughter now has that kettle in a place of honour in her living room. Against the fireplace there were three cast iron oven doors, one on the left side of the fireplace and two above. They were green enameled cast iron. That is where most of the meals were cooked. How Nanny made cakes to rise in them is beyond me. She a made a pound cake every weekend for the grownups. She also had a Primus tabletop stove on our table and she cooked us fried navy beans, and the grownups got fried eggs and bacon.

Across from the kitchen door was a pantry made of stone. Even the shelves where the food was kept were made of stone. There were no fridges or ice boxes. Everything in the pantry was covered with a piece of cheesecloth and flies were everywhere. The pub in the village was also a dairy farm and they would bring the milk to the kitchen window and ladle it out into a jug which was then kept in the pantry. It was delivered every day.

I forgot to tell you about how Nanny had to do the dishes in the big sink in the kitchen with a soap saver. Little bits of carbolic soap were kept for dishes in a wire cage with a handle. The water for the dishes was heated in a kettle on the fireplace hearth. I remember that Nanny used to collect the stickers from the Bisto gravy tins. She stuck them around the outside of the sink. Next to the pantry was a scullery. It was here that my grandmother used to cook the "paunch" (the lining of a cow's stomach). It stunk awful. For a while my grandmother had two Alsatian dogs. The dogs went crazy for it.

From the kitchen there were back stairs that led up to a landing where there was a large bath room and my bedroom. My bedroom was a small room with a bed, dresser, and wardrobe. Across the hall was the night nursery where my cousins used to sleep. Another set of stairs led up to where Nanny slept. I hardly ever went up there as it was ghostly and dark. Outside my bedroom was a door which led to the front landing. The stairs to the kitchen were steep. To save time, I used to jump over the railings and drop to the passage below. I was always in trouble with my grandmother if I was caught.

Just inside the back door there were steps to the cellar where my grandmother grew mushrooms. This was one cold house. I used to get undressed in bed in the winter and put my clothes back on in bed in the morning as there was no heat. I can't believe I lived through it.
I hope this gives you an idea of what the old house was like.

Chapter Two. Christmas at the Rectory

I remember my Christmases as a child in England in the 1930's. As a rule, some of my cousins would be at the rectory where mummy and I lived with my maternal grandparents. Christmas was a gala time with all the children in the village going door- to-door singing carols. This was one of the rare times when I was allowed to mix with them, except for Betty Cook, she was my only friend. For some old fashioned reason it wasn't done for a child from the rectory to play with the village farm children. Different homes would invite us in and we would be given biscuits. On a nice moonlight night we'd all walk down the middle of the road singing carols.

My grandfather always gave a Christmas party in the village hall for the children's choir. That party was a big thing for us children because nothing much ever happened in the village. Every child got a present from the money collected from the carol singing.

Many of the villagers didn't go to church because they didn't like my grandfather who was with the High Church of England. I never saw him practice being High Church. The people who didn't go to church said they were "Chapel folks".

Grandma and Grampa Strudwick

I was, at times, allowed to play with my friend Betty Cook, whose parents ran the post office. They had the only house in the area that had a thatch roof. The Chapel was next door to the post office. But, it was no longer in service. After it had been abandoned Betty Cook and myself were exploring and we had somehow managed to fall through the Chapel's roof. After that time it was never used again.

As well as the party, a nearby village called Halleton would have a Christmas dance. It was three miles away from Slawston. With a group of teens to oversee us, I used to walk to Halleton with the children who grew up with me. We walked the three miles all arm in arm. My nanny would also walk with us during the blackouts in the war years.

In my family, the grandchildren would hang their Christmas stocking up at the end of their beds on Christmas Eve. The next morning we would find them filled with sweets, nuts, and oranges. There would also be a few little toys and always a noise maker. We would then get dressed and go to church, where my grandfather would give Holy Communion.

When we returned from church, we had lunch. Then we were allowed to go into the drawing room where we all lined up in front of a large, blue velvet curtain. When the curtain was opened we saw a beautiful Christmas tree with unlit candles clipped to the branches. Each year, the Christmas tree was a work of art created by mummy.

The rectory had a long driveway dense on either side with a wooded area. The trees were evergreens and chestnut trees. At that time, in this part of England, you weren't allowed to cut down trees. So mummy would use the same wooden bough each year and nail evergreen branches on it in such a way that it formed a proper Christmas tree. It was trimmed with tinsel and ornaments which were the same ones each year. I remember the little birds with white bushy tails clipped onto the tree. They broke very easily.

Also on the tree were the small Victorian candles, clipped onto the branches. The candles were never lit and reused year after year. After we had opened our presents, the village children were allowed in to see the tree. Even though it was the same tree every year, I doubt that any had a tree like the rectory tree.

If we were lucky, we were given two presents. It depended on the value of the gifts. I remember the year 1934. I had turned eight and I received a Bagatelle game. It was a large wooden board with little nails sticking in it and small holes. You had to hit small metal balls with a stick and the balls ran around and would get caught by the nails or fall into the holes, each of which had a score written beside them. That was an expensive gift, so I only received one gift that year. But, from the money collected from Christmas caroling, that same year, the ladies of the village gave me a small doll at the party in the village hall. I remember it was a celluloid doll which had a hand knitted skirt and sweater. I loved that doll. I kept it in my bedroom even as an adult.

We, the children at the rectory for Christmas, were allowed to sit with the grownups in the dining room to listen to the King's speech at 3 pm. We were allowed to take a toy in with us, only on Christmas day, and as usual we were not permitted to speak (children were to be seen and not heard). After the speech ended we went to the kitchen to be with nanny until it was time to be dressed up for Christmas dinner.

I remember the grandeur of the house at Christmas. Mummy and nanny and, of course, us kids would have decorated the house the week before. We put holly across the top of all the pictures. We'd cut the holly from the bushes around the rectory, always being careful to cut the holly bushes so as not to leave gaping holes.

This was one time of the year when nanny, who was also the maid, was expected to wear a pretty white apron and a white headband trimmed with eyelet lace. The rest of the year nanny wore a white starched apron and a white hat similar to a nurse's hat. That tradition was ended during the war years.

Mummy would wear a long, red gown; the same one every year. It was something left over from the twenties. It had a cut-out on the shoulders. As a child, I would see her in that dress and think to myself that she was the most beautiful lady in the world. My grandfather would put on his best suit and my grandmother would wear her best lace gown. My grandmother wore all of her dresses down to the ground every day of the year. She was very Victorian. She wore her hair close to her head in waves and a bun. To me, she always looked the same age. I don't remember her looking any different over time.

I never got along with my grandmother. I was afraid of her most of the time. Believe me, we moved when she raised her voice. She always carried a walking cane with her in the winter and a parasol during the summer. She would move the rectory cats and dogs and tell them, "You don't need to be by the fireplace wearing a fur coat. Go away." Occasionally I also felt the cane on the back of my legs. She was strict but her bark was worse than her bite.

For Christmas, my cousins and I would always put on our best clothes. I had a silky party dress. It was light green with little flowers in the print, with a full skirt, puffed sleeves, and a tiny lace collar. I wore that dress "for best" until I outgrew it. I felt like a princess with my shiny black shoes and long white socks.

We were allowed to use the main staircase that night. The little electric lights were turned on in the hallway only on Christmas night because of the price of electricity. All dressed up, we walked down the stairs into a brilliantly lit hall with none of the ghostly shadows which I saw for the rest of the year. Quietly, we all went into the dining room. Grandfather put the bottle of port wine on the hearth in front of the fireplace to warm it. The grownups would use it to toast King George at the end of the meal. Grandmother would summon nanny (the maid) and she would bring in the goose on a silver platter. Sometime during the war years we began using a turkey at Christmas. The large table was laid by mummy who would place a wide red satin ribbon over the white linen tablecloth. She made it cross in the middle and hang over the table edges to make it look like a present.

On this day the grandchildren were on their best behaviour. It was such a delight to be able to sit with the grownups at such a beautiful table. We didn't make a sound other than when grandfather chose one of us to say the Grace, in Latin. Nanny would serve us and bring in the

Christmas pudding. Grandfather would strike a match and light it up. It gave off a beautiful blue flame. Grandmother would cut the pudding. We also had a Christmas cake that nanny and grandmother had made weeks ahead. It had a layer of almond icing and a layer of white royal icing. On top of the cake sat a porcelain robin on a log. We used the same robin every year. The children had a piece of cake and the grownups had the pudding with the rum in it. We sat and watched the grownups toast the King.

After we all left the table, we went into the drawing room and had to sit silently while the grownups talked and laughed. To me, at Christmas, it was the most beautiful room that I had ever seen, with the beautifully decorated tree in the bay window. I had to sit still and not talk unless I was spoken to. I didn't mind that, it was a wonderland of a day and by that time I would be feeling quite tired. I was allowed to stay up until nine pm. I was always sent to bed before my two cousins, Richard and Brian. Richard was two years older than me and I looked up to him. He was always too old to play with me but his younger brother Brian was only two months older than me so I could never understand why he was allowed to stay up later. I once asked nanny and she scolded me, saying that I was "different", and that grandfather and grandmother had to pay for everything I had. As I had no father in England to support me, she said that I should be grateful that I had a roof over my head at all. This phrase was repeated over and over again throughout my childhood. I also had to be grateful to my uncle because he paid for me to attend an expensive girls 'school run by the nuns. I got so used to being told that phrase, that I just didn't care anymore and eventually I rebelled. But that is another story.

The Cousins
Ann, Brian Cocup, Bonita Sparrow, Richard Cocup
David Sparrow, Sally Cocup

I got used to being treated differently than my cousins. I didn't understand it but, I really didn't care. I was used to being alone. I would lay on my bed and make up stories about growing up to be a rich princess. I would put all my stuffed animals around me and tell them all about it. I used to treat my stuffed animals as if they were real people.

One Christmas my father sent me a present all the way from Canada! It was a baby doll with a Bakelite head. If I ever dropped it, the head would get little surface cracks. It had painted-on eyes and was dressed in a white and pink dress and bonnet. It lay on a pink satin pillow. I still think it was the most beautiful doll I've ever seen. Today I dress dolls for my great grandchildren with this doll in mind.

I hope that I am not making you feel as if you should feel sorry for me. I didn't have a happy childhood by today's standards. But, at that time, I didn't know any different so I didn't feel sorry for myself. I don't remember mummy or nanny ever giving me a kiss or a cuddle. Nanny had always told me, "You were born in Canada so you must be stronger and you don't kiss or hug". Isn't that the silliest thing you've ever heard? I remember my auntie Marjorie going to give me a kiss when she came for a visit. I would cringe and she would laugh and say, "I know Ann, you don't like to be kissed and I don't have the faintest idea why." From the age of five to sixteen I was a loner. Perhaps now my own children will understand why I was awkward when hugging and kissing them.

I do wish that my own children could've experienced a Christmas from that era, they would've learned so much about the magic of an old fashioned Christmas. Christmas at the rectory was always beautiful. I have only wonderful memories of that time.

Mum – Katherine McKay (Strudwick) and Ann

Kenneth (Widdy) McKay – passed away at age 18 months

Grampa Strudwick and Ann

Grampa and Grandma Strudwick
Ann Aunt Brownie Mum
Uncle Jack Strudwick Uncle Raynor Strudwick

Peter, Ann and Billy
Slawston Rectory backyard

Nanny holding David Sparrow, Ann and Bonita Sparrow

Rectory viewed from the tennis court

Ann age 10 and 16

Chapter Three. My Education

My education was something else. In England I went to school in the home of a retired school teacher in the village of Slawston in Leicestershire. I can't remember how long I was with her. Next, my mum sent me to a school in Broadstairs in the south of England, called Miss Oldakers. I was very unhappy there as it was the first boarding school I'd ever been to.

Miss Oldakers was run by two old ladies and their brother. It had boys and girls and was in a large house. I think my grandmother talked my mum into sending me there because I had had very little religion in the past. Believe me, there I got religion morning, noon, and night. I remember my mother sent me a very pretty doll for my birthday. It was wearing clothes which she had knitted herself. The teachers wouldn't let me have it and they kept it on the dressing table and only let me look at it on Sundays; not touch it, just look at it. You have to realize that we had no toys whatsoever. They said toys were a sin. I was very young and I only stayed there for one term as I begged my mother not to send me back there.

Next, my Uncle Dick paid for me to go to a convent boarding school run by Church of England nuns. They were the best years I had had for a long time. It was quite a large school. It was expensive and only girls went there. I had to buy a school uniform, but my grandmother made all of my underwear (bloomers). They were awful and they showed under my skirt. I was to wear only brown shoes. As it happened, one year I hadn't any brown shoes. So, my mother painted my black shoes with brown paint. But, it wore off before the end of the term. For that, I got into trouble, which was nothing new.

I didn't work very hard at my studies. Instead I loved sports and played lacrosse, netball (like basketball), tennis, swimming, gymnastics, and field hockey. I ended up as Captain of my school, but I lost that title because my grades were too low. I had to do a lot of extra studying. If you are at a boarding school the nuns could sock it to you. I got my grades up and was allowed to play sports again (on and off depending on my grades). I also loved crafts, especially the pottery wheel. Of course none of this helped my education. For punishment, I had to stay in and mend socks for the nuns. If they were not done to their liking then they cut the mending out and made me start again. To this day I do a good job on mending socks. The other thing I had to do was learn table manners, which I did very well. I'm very thankful that I can go anywhere and know how to act. I have always loved a properly laid table and good manners. So I learned something we all need in life. But, I began failing again. I can't remember passing any grades and it showed in my spelling. Finally, my Uncle Dick took me out of that school in disgrace.

Then I was sent to a grammar school in Market Halborough with boys and girls. I remember the Latin teacher would walk into the classroom and by the time the door slammed shut, he had hit someone with his walking stick, either for making noise or not sitting straight. I was so afraid of him. I sat at the back of class. I got the walking stick from many teachers, mostly for not doing my homework right. In those days there was no such thing as a slow learner. I think that was my problem, but I did alright in anything I liked to do. They didn't do psychology tests on you in those days. I know I needed extra help and that was unheard of. Any child that had learning problems was considered "just lazy".

After that, another uncle, Leonard, and Uncle Dick got together and I was sent to St Katherine and St Helen, a boarding school in Abington, Berkshire. Both schools were joined together, so I saw some of the girls that I already knew. I had a problem there because I had very little pocket money. I talked a day girl (non-boarder) into giving me some of her sweets (candy). Well that was not allowed and a nun saw me with a sweet in my mouth, so I was put in conbertory (which meant no one was allowed to talk to me for a week). When you are away from home, that is rough and you get very lonely. I finally tried to learn my bookwork but, I was so far behind on everything. It was too late. I am afraid that everyone gave up on me, including my family.
So I was taken out of school again and sent to a different boarding school in Broadstairs. It was just after the war had broken out and since Broadstairs is on the English Channel coast, it was not the safest place to be. The school had both boys and girls. Some were Jewish refugees from Europe. I remember one small boy who hadn't seen his parents for quite a while. Finally, his parents escaped from Poland and arrived to get him. This was the time when Germany had taken over Poland.

That school was awful. I had to write to my mother every Sunday. But my letters were read aloud to the teacher who made me do it again if I wrote anything against the school. In that half term I got at least four strappings for something or another. I wasn't allowed to tell anyone. My mum would write to me and would ask me direct questions, and as I didn't answer them she caught on that something was wrong. Mum requested that I be sent home at once. I was put on a train at Broadstairs station and met in London by my mother. When I told her what had happened to me, mum was angry at my grandmother for ever talking her into sending me there. Well, that was the end of schooling for me. So at 14, I left school with next to nothing for an education. You could leave school at 14 in those days. That was when I started working in factories for the war effort. Now I feel sorry for my mother because it caused a rift between her and her mother. My grandmother never liked me anyway. I guess it was because I never conformed to her ways. My cousins, Brian and Richard, both did very well in school and grew up with good jobs; as did the rest of my cousins. I was the black sheep and not forgiven. Even Nanny didn't mind rubbing it in at times but I must say that Nanny treated me the best of everybody.

Ann age 14

So much for my education. I didn't tell my children about this because I wanted more for my children than I had. Forgive me, my girls for not having told you the truth about my education for all these years.

Chapter Four. The War Years

The war broke out when I was 13 years old. I was a long-legged, scrawny kid with pigtails down to my waist. The day the war broke out I was at Hoylake, a seaside town on the Mersey. To get to Hoylake we had to take a tube (subway) train from Liverpool to where the train line ended at a place called Meols. Hoylake is where my Aunt Marjorie, who everyone called Miggs, lived. She was my dad's sister. She had two boys and a girl. The two boys, my cousins, were named John and Tommy. Both served as officers in the Merchant Navy during the war years. Her daughter was named Peggy and she was a lot younger than me.

Ann age 13 Hoylake on the Mersey

My Auntie Miggs was good to me. She is the one who gave me my bike. It had Dynamo lights on the front and the back; no batteries needed. The more you peddled the brighter the light would shine. Why we don't have them today is beyond me.

I spent my holidays at the home of Auntie Miggs and her husband, Uncle Bar (short for Barton Mothersille). When the war broke out, my uncle Bar returned to Canada (as he was a Canadian) to join the Essex Scottish Regiment in Windsor, Ontario. His rank was a Major and because of his older age he did not go to Dieppe. But his younger brother, Jack Mothersille, did. He was a Captain and was taken as a Prisoner of War by the Germans. Uncle Jack spent the rest of the war in a German prison. I met him after the war at Auntie Miggs. He must have had a hard time because he looked terrible. I don't think he lived many years after that.

At that time, Auntie Miggs had a maid. I don't remember her name but she had a boyfriend who joined the Hoylake Squadron. It was made up of a group of men from the Home Guard. They had very little training. Remember, this is the year war broke out, and we didn't have much of an army at that time. He was a Private, with little training, and was sent overseas very soon after joining. I went with the family to see him off, not knowing that would be the last time we would ever see him. He was killed in France.

In 1942 I spent Christmas at Hoylake. My poor Auntie Miggs had quite a time with her own three children and I didn't help much. At that time, Liverpool and Birkenhead were getting blitzed by the Germans. So my Auntie Miggs had a bomb shelter put in the dining room. The dining room table was taken out and was replaced with a heavy steel cage-like shelter. It had wire bars around it. She kept bedding in it and as soon as the air raid sirens would sound, we kids were told to get out of bed and stay in the cage. Quite a lot of German planes were shot down before they got to the big city of Liverpool, so they would drop their bombs over Hoylake whilst going up over the River Mersey. Liverpool also had barrage balloons up to keep the German planes up high. They also had to go through the British Ack Ack guns.

As you might guess, John, and Tommy, and myself didn't stay put and we used to sneak outside to see the action. It was something, to see the searchlights locking on planes then trying to shoot them down with Ack Ack guns. The sky was lit up like daylight. That is where I got my piece of shrapnel from: one of our British Ack Ack guns. After all, what goes up, must come down. Shrapnel goes red hot and if you are not wearing a tin hat it will kill you. My poor Auntie Miggs would have a fit and make us go indoors. As a kid I was not a bit afraid. I guess it was my age, plus not much sense in my head.

In Liverpool and Birkenhead, as soon as the air raid sirens would sound, the people all had to go down into the tube (subway) stations where steel bunk beds were lined up along the walls. This went on for at least two years. The poor little kids had little time to sleep in their own beds. This was happening all over England. I know you have heard the song, The White Cliffs of Dover. The part that says, "and Jimmy will go to sleep in his own little bed again", this is what it meant.

At home in Leicester I lived in digs, (rented rooms), with my mother. She worked as a bookkeeper for civilian men working for the army. I joined the ARP as a messenger. When the siren went off, I would get out of bed, put on the navy blue uniform, put on the tin hat over my curlers, and go down to the air raid shelter. I would make tea for the firefighters and wardens. We were trained so that if all the telephone lines went down, we would take messages on our bikes. As I recall, Leicester only had one air raid and I was lead to believe that it was a mistake by the Germans.

At that time, Leicester had no defenses in the city. We were under the impression that we had Ack Ack guns in the park. We could see them and couldn't understand why they were not used during the one and only air raid. We found out later that they were made of wood to fool the enemy. They were blocked off and you could only see them from the road. They really did look real. I was given to understand that same thing happened all over England at the beginning of the war. So all I did in the ARP was train, route march, and make tea.

At the time, I was in a boarding school. At 14, I left school. If you were not in school, you either went to College or went to a factory to help with the war effort. I worked in an aircraft factory in Market Harborough. I worked the day shift, sixty hours a week, on a drilling machine and a tapping machine. A short time later, I went to a machine shop called Jones and Shipman (now called Jones, Shipman and Harding). I worked on a lathe and then a milling machine, still doing sixty hours a week. Can you picture me, a young girl just out of a convent boarding school, working with a rough bunch of millwrights? Boy I learned a lot of new words and a lot about life. Because of that, I begged my mother to let me join up. At that time I was only 17 and had to have a parent's permission. My mother was not too happy with the war at the time and suggested I join the Land Army. But, I couldn't picture myself wearing breeches, a blouse and a thick green sweater to work on a farm. To make it worse, many farmers had POW's from Italy working on their farms. Also, most farmers didn't like women working on their farms. I knew I wouldn't be happy doing that. It sounded like no fun.

Without telling mum, I went to the recruiting centre to join the WAAF (Women's Auxiliary Air Force). I lied about my age and got as far as the date to have a medical. That was when they found out I had not been given permission by my mother. I got a letter telling me to come back in a year. From there, I talked her into letting me join the ATS (Auxiliary Territorial Service), the women's army corps. Off I went to the recruiting office and applied with my mother's permission. In the office where my mother worked were several ATS drivers. They sat me down and told me all about the army, and that sure put me off of joining. I don't think they were very happy campers.

Uncle Dick Cocup and Brian Cocup

Back to the recruiting office I went, and saw a very nasty sergeant. She told me off good and proper for wasting her time. Back to the factory life I went. I began to think about the Navy, as that was all that was left. That was at the bottom of my list. You see, I already had cousins in the Royal Navy. Brian Cocup RN, who went through Dartmouth, started as a cadet and by this time was a sub lieutenant. His brother, Richard, was also in the Navy, serving as an officer in the RNR (Royal Navy Reserve). If I joined I would be a WREN. But, I would have no rank as I didn't finish school. I didn't feel like taking humble pie from them. I was 17 and a half when I finally did join the Navy.

Ann Day

I was called up to go to Mill Hill, London, just before my 18th birthday. For two weeks I scrubbed floors, did dishes, and marched on the parade grounds, etc. At that time the V2's were going over London. I was scared and used to pull the covers over my head. What good that did I don't know. If they hit, I would be dead anyway. But, being young, very little bothered me. From there I was sent up to Greenock, Scotland. Being a skivvy, I hauled potatoes on my back from the docks. I was up at dawn in the kitchen helping the cook. It was a lousy job. I was there for New Year's, 1944. At the Wrenery, we put on a dance and invited the sailors on the HMCS (His Majesty's Canadian Ship) Puncher. It was known as a banana boat (a corvette boat converted from a tanker). Wouldn't you know it, there was one sailor aboard who was an Englishman. He worked in radar. I went out with him for the rest of my time in the Navy. He was transferred to a Royal Navy destroyer, the Oribi (pennant number G66) and I didn't see very much of him as he was on convoy duty. I was given leave and hitchhiked home for 10 days.

WREN friends

At that time my mother was still working for the army, and living at the rectory at Slawston, a small village outside of Market Harborough. She drove a small Austin car. It was built before the war and had no windshield wipers. The seats were leather and had snappers which you opened to inflate the cushion inside the seat. It also had a sunroof. During the blackouts, cars travelling after dark had to have their headlights covered with black cardboard to let out only the smallest possible amount of light. So, when it rained at night, the only way you could drive was to have someone walk in front of the car to ensure the way was clear. When I was with mum that was my job. How would you like to walk fifteen miles in front of a car in the pouring rain? The blackout was necessary because if any light was seen by the German bombers that became a target for their bombs. They came over the English countryside every night, flying in droves, very high. The drone of the engine sounded like it was saying repeatedly "you, you, you, you, you". It wasn't pleasant to hear.

One night before I joined up, we heard such a noise at the rectory. It was the Americans parachuting from planes, practicing for D-day. They missed their mark, landing in the middle of the village instead of landing in the farmers 'fields. We found it very interesting. Nanny and mom invited them in for a cup of tea. That was how I got my first ride in a Jeep. I went with two Yankees to help pick up parachutes around the village. I was the envy of the village girls.

One thing I forgot to tell my readers about was the time that the Battle of Britain was going on. At that time, we used to tune in at 12 noon on our shortwave radio and listen to what we called "Lord Haw Haw". He was a German who broadcast every day telling the English how many planes the Germans had shot down. He never told the truth. We would get the truth from the 6 pm British news. Nobody ever believed him, but we did believe him when he told us what was going to happen to the English people after Germany invaded us. He said that all the old and sick people were to be killed. Young men would work in camps for Germany. All the young women would be sent to Germany to breed an elite population.

We were, quite literally, fighting for our lives. The Americans were sending tanks etc., to help but, officially, they weren't in the war. In the event that that the Germans succeeded in invading Britain, my mother had a plan. She was in charge of a prescription for morphine for my aunt, her sister, who was dying of breast cancer. She was only 32 years old. Sadly, she died at the rectory leaving behind two children, my cousins, Benito, and her younger brother, David. If the Germans invaded Britain, my mother planned to make a big pot of tea and had arranged with my grandmother to lace the tea with morphine. All of us would drink the tea because death would be better than letting the Germans get any of us. Well you all know your history. Luckily, Germany didn't invade, as Hitler had the Russians on another front and that changed his mind. As a WREN, I was sent to Liverpool to work in the Royal Liver Building as a messenger. This was the building where all the ship convoys were planned. I did get to see the room where the navy maps were laid out on a big table and they mapped out and planned the Atlantic crossings. I found it very interesting. As a messenger, I was given a pass to enter the areas that were "top secret"; not that I understood much of what was going on. But, I did see the large table with small toy-like ships on it, being pushed with a long pole by officers.

HMS Rodney battleship firing guns

Then I was transferred to Woodvale, not far from Liverpool, to the Fleet Air Arm (a Navy airport). I worked there as a messenger. I also worked in the ward room known as the Officers Mess. I worked behind the counter seeing that the pilots that came in had somewhere to sleep. It was during this time that I saw my first jet. I was at Woodvale on VJ Day (the day the Japanese surrendered). On VE Day (the end of the war with Germany), I was on Leave in Leicester. I got a little drunk.

I haven't told you of my two uncles who were naval chaplains. My mother's younger sister married Leonard Coulshaw who ended up as Chaplain for the Fleet, a position that carried an Admiral's rank. He was also chaplain to the King. My other uncle, Dick, married my mother's other sister (she had 3 sisters and 2 brothers). My Uncle Dick pulled a few strings to get me out of the Navy as soon as the war ended, to return to Canada. I was sent to a disperse station outside of Redding to wait for my demobilization. I should've had two more years to put in before my release but, somehow Uncle Dick got me out on April 22, 1946.

Uncle Dick   Uncle Leonard

Uncle Dick was Chaplain on the HMS Hood and fortunately was on leave at the time the German battleship Bismarck sank the Hood.

Uncle Leonard was Chaplain of the Royal Navy Fleet, highest Chaplain rank in the Royal Navy during World War II

I returned to civilian life while waiting to leave England. I went to work for the Post Office as a long distance switchboard operator The Post Office was the telephone company owned by the government. This was in 1946 and that was the year I first saw a TV set. It was also the first time I saw a plastic bowl and plastic baby pants; until then they were made of rubber.

Everything was still rationed. I won't get into that because you would wonder how people survived in those days. The rationing in Canada was nothing compared to what it was like in England. It was nice to be able to take down the blackout drapes and let the light come in from outside.

The sailor I met from the Puncher was still around and wanted me to marry him. He was from Milton, in the Lake District. His family was from generations of coal miners. I was young and in love, unaware of the risks miners took, and I said I didn't care that they were a mining family. My mother did care however and she made me a deal: I would go to Canada with her to live with my dad for one year. If I still wanted to marry my sailor at the end of that year, then she would send me back to England. As I hadn't seen my dad since I was four years old, I took her up on it. When we said goodbye, I think he knew I would not return. We called each other only a few times and I knew he would not come to Canada. I was broken-hearted for a while. But, I got over him.

Chapter Five. My Ship from Southampton to New York 1946

In 1945, my uncle, Dick Cocup, managed to get my mother and myself out of England and back to Canada. During the war my uncle, who was a Royal Navy chaplain, gave his ration of whiskey to a US Naval officer. This friend was able to get mum and myself a birth on board an American ship, called "The Washington". It was still in troop condition but, at the time, it was just about impossible to get a birth on ANY ship. The ship was headed to New York and, from there, we would make our way home to Windsor, Ontario.

Mum and I had to go to London to get our passports up to date. Again, because of Uncle Dick, we didn't have to go through the usual channels and line ups (it's not "what" you know, it's "who" you know). We saw a great big lineup on the street outside of the emigration building, all doing the same in order to leave the country.

When everything was in order, we travelled to Southhampton to await the arrival of the ship. We visited with my cousin, Brian Cocup, and met his wife, Wendy, as they were living in Southampton.

The "Washington" was still in wartime condition. Cabins on one side of the ship were for men and the other side for women. It had a few staterooms but not as you know them today. They were made up for four people but, again, either for males or females. As it was August, couples and families who wished to be together slept on the deck. Mum and I were lucky to get a stateroom, thanks to Uncle Dick and his friend. The condition the other people had to travel in was awful; even more so below deck. The two ladies we shared the stateroom with were very nice. They were returning to their homes in America. They had been in England when the war broke out and were not able to return home until it ended.

Most of the people on the ship were from Europe. Some were French as the ship had been in La Harve, France, before it docked in Southampton. Very few of the Europeans spoke English and I thought they were a loud bunch, with no manners. They all seemed to be wearing a lot of diamonds and gold. I found out later that, during the war, they had buried jewelry and valuable in their gardens for safekeeping. When the war ended, they sold everything and turned any money they had into gold to wear, in order to get it into the States.

My mum with her Oxford English accent managed to make friends with three American gentlemen. They kept to themselves away on a private deck. My mother played poker with them for pennies. One was a Mr. Dale, who we later found out was a millionaire who owned a Hawaiian island! Another was Mr. Forbes, the publisher, who was also a millionaire. The third man always had two other men sitting near him. We later found out that they were FBI agents because the third man was Herbert Hoover, head of the FBI. It was all very "hush hush". I was very impressed that they allowed my mum on that deck. No one else was allowed up there except for the stewards. Mr. Hoover wouldn't admit to my mother who he was. She told him she had recognized him right away. He just laughed. He was a pleasant man to talk with. He used to kid me about finding a boyfriend on the ship. He joked a lot, as did the other two millionaires. At the end of the sailing, before we docked in New York, a launch came alongside of our ship, with more men aboard. Mr. Hoover left with them and the two FBI escorts. We never saw any of the three millionaires again. But, when we got home, we read in the Windsor Star newspaper that Herbert Hoover had arrived back in New York from London, safely by ship. So, mum was right.

During the voyage, I didn't have anyone to speak to as it seemed few other people spoke English. Most of the other passengers were, I was told, refugees who had been granted US citizenship and only had a certain time to get to the States in order to keep their citizenship. Also on that trip I met a survivor of Bergen Belsen, a concentration camp in Poland. She was a young girl, now a US citizen, with a nun looking after her. When the weather was sunny she was brought up on the deck. She looked terrible. It was hard to guess her age. I would say she was a teenager. She was skinny and sickly looking, gaunt and seemed frightened. The nun told me about her. It was all very sad.

I had a bad trip. I was sea sick from Southampton to Ireland, where we weighed anchor to take on a group of Irish people. Once the engine on the ship stopped I felt a lot better and walked around to look at all the people. But, as soon as the screw (engine) started up again, I got sick again. It was awful because the ship had the greatest food; things which I hadn't seen during the war years. But, I felt too sick to eat. Mum would bring me watermelon and it was all I could eat.

The trip took seven days at around twenty knots. On the fifth day I saw the ship's doctor and he gave me Gravol pills which helped. Finally, on the last night aboard, my poor mum slipped in the shower and got a black eye. I felt sorry for her as she worried about meeting my dad again looking like that.

The trip up the Hudson River into New York was something to see with the Statue of Liberty and the skyline. We dropped anchor at Ellis Island and were told to line up for the immigration officers who were sitting at tables. The people were awful, pushing and shoving and yelling at one another. My mother said we should wait and not get in the line with them. So we stepped out of the line and waited. Eventually we went to the immigration officer. My mum said, "I bet you are tired after that mob." He said, "Yes I am". He must've had quite a time because he was crabby with us and he gave us only twelve hours to get out of the USA, as her passport was British and was stamped to go to Canada.

We got a cab at the docks to take us to Grand Central Station. The cab driver tried to make an extra buck by taking us the long way around. He didn't realize that my mum had lived in the States before. She gave him hell and refused to give him a tip. I nearly died of embarrassment (it didn't take much being a teenager).

When we got into the station, mum realized that she didn't have any more American money (only British and Canadian). It was nearly 3pm and, at that time, all the banks closed at 3 pm. We dashed outside and ran to a bank on the corner. It was just closing. Mum banged on the glass door and explained our money problem. The security guard got the manager and he listened to our story and let us in and changed our British pounds to US dollars. We were very grateful. While we waited the four hours for our train, I had my first ice cream since the beginning of the war.

We had a sleeping birth on the train as we were travelling all night. Mum asked the porter to wake us up before we got into Windsor. But, somehow, he forgot. We were asleep when we arrived at the Windsor station, so we had to rush to get dressed and out of the train before it left the station. Unfortunately, my mum had taken off her pearls the night before and she left them in the little safekeeping hammock on the train. It was a real pearl necklace, worth a few dollars, and we never saw it again.

My dad and his sister, Aunt Kath, met us at the station. My mum felt awful. She hadn't seen my dad for all these years and there she was with a black eye, wearing no make-up, and of course she had wanted to look so nice. Well that was an unbelievable trip to end our war years.

About the author.
Ann Day was born in 1927. She now lives in Canada. Her memoire's are vivid and comical. A delightful depiction of life in the 1930's & as well in the 1940's.

Printed in Great Britain
by Amazon